Ukulele
for
Kids

By Mark Daniels

A Fun and Easy
Way to Learn

ISBN-13: 978-1522775140
ISBN-10: 1522775145
Ukulele for Kids: A Fun and Easy Way to Learn

Contents

The Ukulele Explained

Take a look at your ukulele. It's pretty cool isn't it? I will tell you a little secret that no other ukulele teacher knows. Your ukulele wants you to play it. It wants you to pick it up and make some noise with it. If your ukulele had a mouth, it would be smiling every time it was in your hands. Go ahead and play around with it. Just make some noise with it. Make your ukulele happy!

Your ukulele might look a little different and that's okay because there are several different types of ukuleles out there. Yours might be a different color or it could be a different size. You might even have one that is a different shape. I have a ukulele that is shaped like a pineapple!

Pineapple Shaped Ukulele

I like to think of my ukulele as having three sections or pieces. Kind of like a pizza but without the cheese and pepperoni. My ukulele has a Body, a Neck and a Headstock. So does yours. This picture should help you understand.

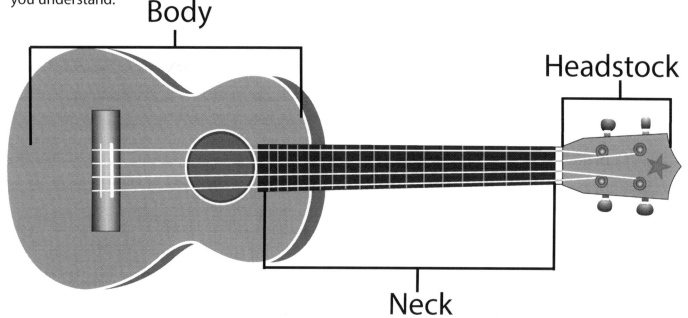

Body

Headstock

Neck

Headstock

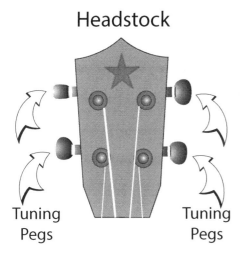

Let's take a closer look at the top piece or Headstock. This is the part of your ukulele that lets you keep everything in tune. Don't worry. The headstock on your ukulele may look a little different than mine. It's okay because most headstocks do look different.

See those shiny knobby looking things? Those are called TUNING PEGS and they are almost like magic because they let you change the pitch of each string on your ukulele. You have to be really gentle with these because if you turn them too far in the wrong direction, you will break a string and that is no fun!

Tuning Pegs   Tuning Pegs

Notice how there is one tuning peg for every string on your ukulele? That is because each tuning peg controls the pitch of its very own string.

Turning the tuning peg in one direction will tighten the string and make the pitch of the string go higher. Turning the tuning peg in the opposite direction will loosen the string and make the pitch of the string go lower. Don't turn any of these yet.

Neck

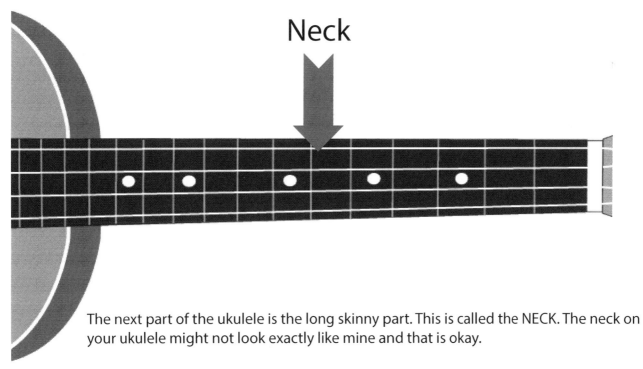

The next part of the ukulele is the long skinny part. This is called the NECK. The neck on your ukulele might not look exactly like mine and that is okay.

This is the part of the ukulele where your left hand will be playing and dancing. Go ahead and take a closer look at the NECK. Get up close and look at it. Move your hands over the strings.

Does the neck of your ukulele have spots like mine does? These help you keep track of where your hand is and where it needs to go when you start playing your ukulele. Not all ukulele necks have spots. Some of them have squares, rectangles or triangles.

Do you see those little metal bars all over the neck? Those are called frets. A different note lives between each fret.

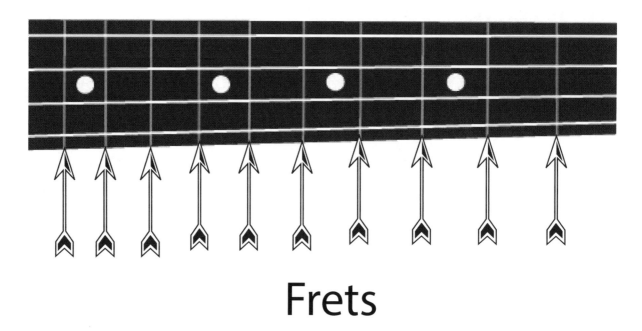

Frets

As you move up the neck towards the BODY of the ukulele the notes get higher in pitch. That is how you get those really high pitched notes that have been known to break glass.

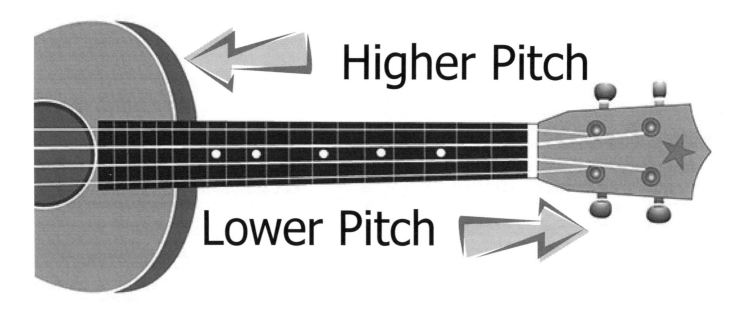

The part of the neck where your fingers hold down the strings is called the fretboard. This is where your fingers become one with your ukulele and beautiful music happens.

The next part of the ukulele is the BODY. This is the biggest part of the ukulele. Go ahead and check it out. What's the first thing you see? I can't help but notice that giant hole right in the middle.

Sound Hole

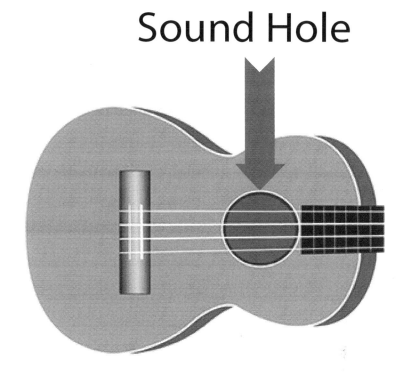

Don't worry, your ukulele is not broken. It is supposed to have a big hole in the middle of the BODY. This hole is called the sound hole. Let's see if the sound hole is working correctly.

Get as close to the sound hole as you can. Take a peek inside. Now comes the fun part. Put your mouth close to the sound hole and yell, scream or sing right into the hole.

Did you notice how your voice sounded different. It sounded bigger didn't it? This means the sound hole on your ukulele is working.

That hole makes the sound of your strings louder. Without the sound hole, your ukulele would be so quiet a mouse couldn't even hear it.

There is one more part on the BODY. It is called the BRIDGE.

This is where the strings start on your ukulele. You can follow them all the way up the NECK until they reach the tuning pegs on the HEADSTOCK.

Congratulations my ukulele playing friend. You now know what each part of the ukulele is for. It is almost time to make some beautiful music!

Bridge

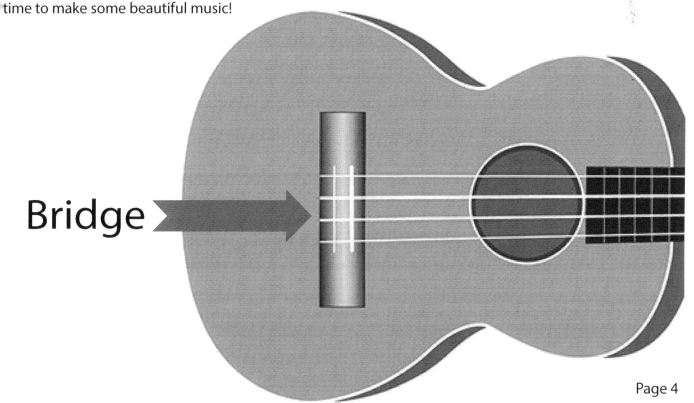

The Strings

Let's take a closer look at the strings on your ukulele. There should be four of them. Look at them really close. Each string is a little different isn't it? The string at the very top and the very bottom are thinner than the two strings in the middle. They all sound different too.

In order to make things easier to understand, the ukulele strings have been numbered. The string at the very bottom is the First string. The next string is called the second and then the third and the fourth. This picture should make it easy to understand.

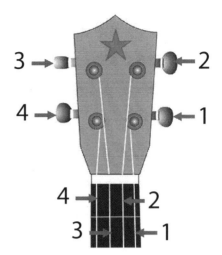

Using your thumb, lightly pluck the top or FOURTH string. Listen to it. It sounds pretty cool doesn't it? Believe it or not, you just made music. Congratulations!

When you pluck a string without your playing hand pressing it down anywhere on the neck of your ukulele, this is called playing an OPEN string. It is open because your fingers are not holding it down on the fretboard.

Use the palm of your hand to mute the strings. Just rest your hand on the strings like this. Notice how the sound stops? This is a quick and easy way to keep your ukulele quiet.

Move your thumb over the next string or the THIRD string and lightly pluck it. You just made music again! Notice how this string sounds different? It is lower in pitch. Use the palm of your hand to mute the strings again.

Use your thumb to lightly pluck each string and listen to the way they sound. As you work your way down the strings pay close attention to the sound. The sound should change with each string. The thicker strings create musical notes that are lower in pitch while the thinner strings create musical notes that are higher in pitch.

Each string also sings a musical note when played open.

The FOURTH string is a G note.
The THIRD string is a C note.
The SECOND string is an E note.
The FIRST string is an A note.

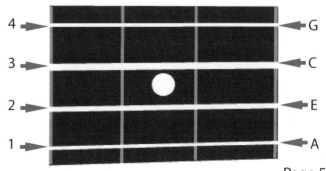

Tuning Your Ukulele

If your parents aren't already helping you with this book and your ukulele, then go get them. Tell them you need help learning how to tune your ukulele.

Did you get your parents? Are they sitting there reading this with you? Awesome! It is time to learn how to tune a ukulele. You know what they say. You can tune a Ukulele but you can't tuna fish!

Parents, help your child with this part. Most kids are not ready to learn how to tune a ukulele when they first start playing.

It takes a little while to understand when a ukulele is in or out of tune. If the ukulele is not in tune, it won't sound too good. Learning how to tune a ukulele is very important and easy if you follow these instructions.

Tuning your ukulele will be so much easier if you have an electronic tuner. I highly recommend a clip on tuner. The tuner I am going to be using for this example is the Fender FT-004. At the time of this writing, this tuner was less than $10.00 at Amazon. It even comes with a battery.

Front View of Tuner

Digital Display

Power / Mode Button

These little tuners are like magic and they make tuning any stringed instrument super easy. You can use it to tune a ukulele, a violin, a guitar, a cello or a bass guitar but you can't use it to tuna fish. Did I just use that old joke again? Sorry about that.

Each time you pluck a string, vibrations travel through every part of your ukulele. Clip on tuners use these vibrations to help you know what musical note each string currently is. Cool huh?

Side View of Tuner

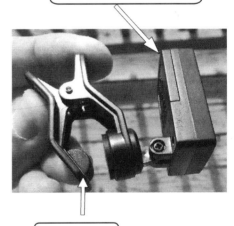

Battery Door

Clip

This tuner is called a clip on tuner because it easily clips on to the headstock of your ukulele like this.

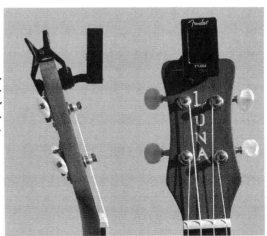

Now let's take a closer look at the digital display. This is where all the magic will be happening.

There is a lot of stuff on the screen of your tuner isn't there? The example image shows the 1ST STRING or A string in perfect tune!

The little 1 in the bottom left of the display tells you which string you are trying to tune. In this example, it is the FIRST STRING. The U in the bottom right of the display tells you which mode is currently selected. In this example, we are tuning a ukulele. U stands for Ukulele.

If your tuner doesn't show a U in the bottom right corner of the display, then lightly press the power mode button. If you hold this button in, the tuner will shut off. If you press the button quickly, you will change tuning modes. Simple and easy! Press it to change the mode until it shows a letter U in the bottom right corner of the display.

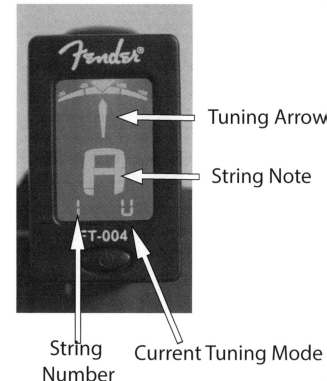

Tuning Arrow

String Note

String Number   Current Tuning Mode

The GIANT A in the middle of the display tells you which note the string is supposed to be. If the note is out of tune, the screen will be blue. The screen changes to green once the string is in tune.

The tuning arrow will help guide you. It will tell you if the pitch of the current string is too low or too high. If the arrow is on the left side of the display, the pitch is too low. If the arrow is on the right side of the display, the pitch is too high. When the arrow is in the middle of the display, the pitch is perfect! Here are some good examples.

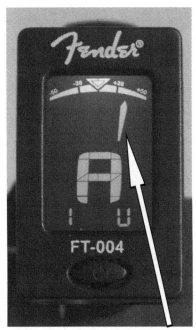

Tuning arrow on the right side of the display. The pitch is too high.

Tuning arrow on the left side of the display. The pitch is too low.

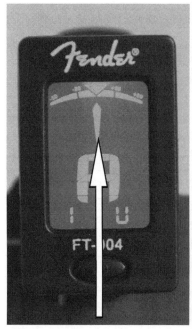

Tuning arrow is in the middle of the display. The pitch is perfect.

All right! Now that you know how the tuner works, let's put everything you just learned into action. It's time to tune your ukulele and with the help of your tuner, it will be simple!

It may be easier for you to lay your ukulele on your lap. This way you can easily see the tuner, strum the ukulele string and turn the tuning peg at the same time.

Make sure your tuner is clipped to the headstock of your ukulele, the power is on and the tuner is in UKULELE mode. There should be a U in the lower right corner of the display.

Let's start by tuning the G or FOURTH string.

Fourth String

Fourth string tuning peg.

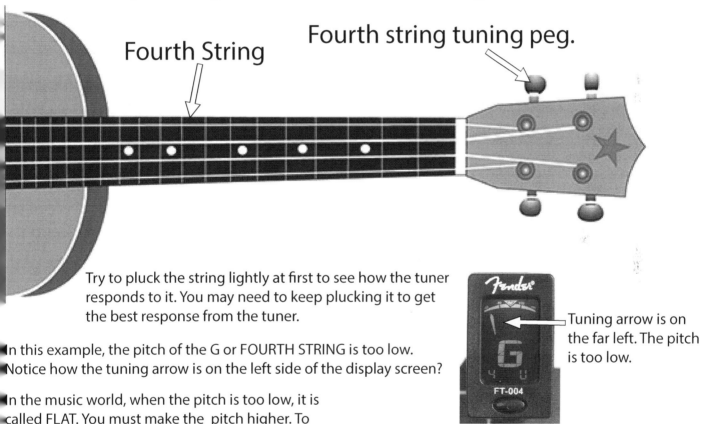

Try to pluck the string lightly at first to see how the tuner responds to it. You may need to keep plucking it to get the best response from the tuner.

In this example, the pitch of the G or FOURTH STRING is too low. Notice how the tuning arrow is on the left side of the display screen?

In the music world, when the pitch is too low, it is called FLAT. You must make the pitch higher. To make the pitch higher on my ukulele, I turn the tuning peg counter clockwise.

Tuning arrow is on the far left. The pitch is too low.

Keep slowly turning the tuning peg until the tuning arrow on the display screen reaches the middle. You might need to keep plucking the G or FOURTH string in order to get the tuner to respond while you are turning the tuning peg. Don't be afraid to ask your parents to help you with this!

Tuning arrow is in the middle. The FOURTH or G string is perfectly tuned.

Now the G or FOURTH STRING is perfectly tuned! Let's tune the next string.

Let's tune the C or THIRD string.

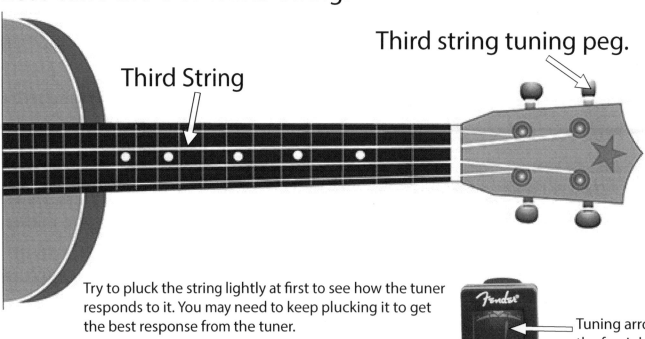

Third String

Third string tuning peg.

Try to pluck the string lightly at first to see how the tuner responds to it. You may need to keep plucking it to get the best response from the tuner.

Tuning arrow is on the far right. The pitch is too high.

In this example, the pitch of the C or THIRD STRING is too high. Notice how the tuning arrow is on the right side of the display screen?

In the music world, when the pitch is too high, it is called SHARP. You must make the pitch LOWER. To make the pitch LOWER on my ukulele, I turn the tuning peg clockwise.

Keep slowly turning the tuning peg until the tuning arrow on the display screen reaches the middle. You might need to keep plucking the C or THIRD string in order to get the tuner to respond while you are turning the tuning peg. Don't be afraid to ask your parents to help you with this!

Now the C or THIRD STRING is perfectly tuned! Now all you need to do is repeat this process for the rest of the strings on your ukulele.

The SECOND string should be tuned to E.
The FIRST string should be tuned to A.

Tuning arrow is in the middle. The THIRD or C string is perfectly tuned.

When you are done, go back and make sure all of the strings stayed in tune. Sometimes they will come out of tune when you are tuning the other strings. If you notice that your ukulele strings are constantly coming out of tune, give it a little time. Brand new ukulele strings stretch. Once they are done stretching, the ukulele will stay in tune for longer periods of time.

I put new strings on one of my ukuleles and it took almost two weeks for the strings to stretch and finally settle in place. Once they did, my ukulele stayed in perfect tune.

Tuning Your Ukulele With A Piano or Electronic Keyboard

You don't have to use a tuner to tune your ukulele. You can always tune your ukulele using a piano or a keyboard. This method of tuning your ukulele is a little harder than using an electronic tuner because you have to match the pitch of your ukulele to the pitch of your piano.

First you will need to locate the notes on the piano. Use this handy image.

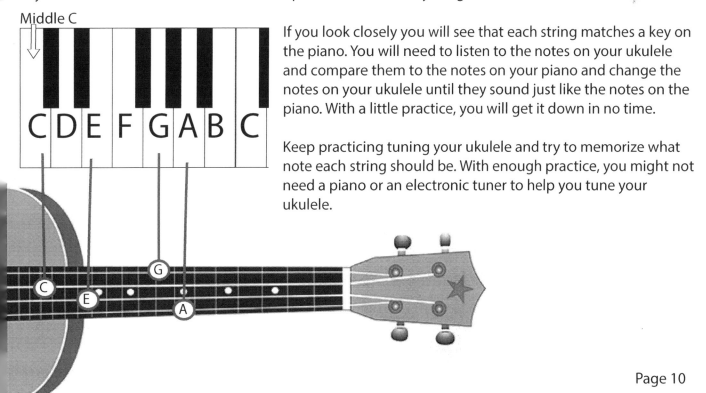

If you look closely you will see that each string matches a key on the piano. You will need to listen to the notes on your ukulele and compare them to the notes on your piano and change the notes on your ukulele until they sound just like the notes on the piano. With a little practice, you will get it down in no time.

Keep practicing tuning your ukulele and try to memorize what note each string should be. With enough practice, you might not need a piano or an electronic tuner to help you tune your ukulele.

 # Holding Your Ukulele

Holding your ukulele the correct way is very important. When you strum or pluck the strings of your ukulele, the vibrations from the strings move through the neck, the body and the headstock. These vibrations are the sounds you hear. The vibrations are music! Holding the ukulele incorrectly stops those vibrations and makes the ukulele very, very quiet. It might be so quiet that even a mouse can't hear it. When you hold your ukulele correctly, the vibrations can travel through the entire ukulele and make loud beautiful music. You want your ukulele to sing loud and proud.

Let's start off by holding your ukulele while sitting down. You can play standing up, but it is easier to learn how to play sitting down. You can sit on a couch, a bed or a chair with no arms. You can even sit on the floor, but it won't be as comfortable.

Relax and get comfortable in your seat, but don't slouch! Slouching is bad for your back and it makes playing your new ukulele even harder. Sit up straight and hold your ukulele like this.

Use your left hand to hold the neck. Rest the top of the body against your belly and use your right arm to hold the ukulele against your body. Don't squish the ukulele with your arm. Use your arm to hold it lightly in place. Remember, you don't want to stop the vibrations by holding the ukulele too tightly.

The main goal of holding your ukulele is comfort. Relax and sit as comfortable as possible.

Here is what holding your ukulele looks like if you were to look straight down. Only a small portion of your arm is holding the ukulele against your ribs.

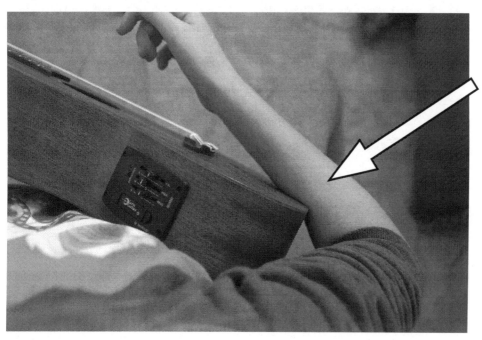

Using Your Hands As A Team

Before you start strumming your ukulele and making beautiful music, you need to learn where and how you will be using your hands. This part of the book is for people who write with their right hand. If you are left handed, you will need a special "lefty" ukulele. Don't worry. I am not going to leave the leftys out. They need to learn how to play too!

Here is another secret most ukulele teachers never tell their students. Your hands will be working together like a team. One hand will be doing all the strumming while the other hand moves and dances all over the neck. It may seem like they are doing different things, but they will actually be working together to make beautiful music.

Your right hand has now been magically transformed into your STRUMMING HAND. Your left hand is important too. Let's make it part of the team. Let's call it THE PLAYING HAND. Your PLAYING HAND will be used to hold down the strings on the fret board. You will only be using four fingers on the fret board. Your thumb will rest on the back of the neck and help you keep your hand steady.

For all of you leftys out there that feel the need to hold a ukuelele in their hands and make magical music, you will be doing everything the opposite of the right handers out there. Your left hand will be doing all of the strumming. Your left hand will now become your STRUMMING HAND.

Your right hand needs to be part of the team. Your right hand will be dancing and jumping around on the neck of the ukulele while your left hand does all of the strumming.

Strumming for the First Time

What? You haven't already strummed your ukulele? Let's get to it and make some magic happen.

Strumming is easy, but you can do it wrong. Strumming the wrong way could break the strings on your ukulele and strumming the wrong way will knock your ukulele out of tune. Strumming should be nice and easy. Don't pull the strings and don't dig your strumming finger into them either.

If you are right handed, then forget about your left hand for a minute. Leftys, you need to forget about your right hand for a minute. We are only going to be using our STRUMMING hand.

Your index or pointing finger will become your strumming finger and you will be strumming the ukulele where the neck meets the body.

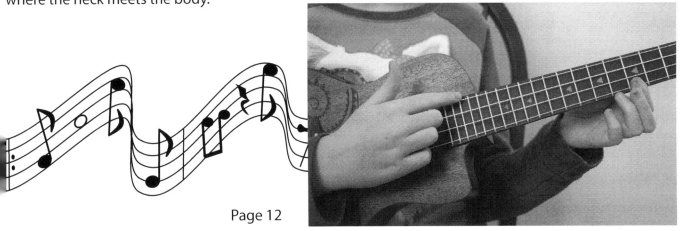

I find it easier to strum a little further up on the neck of the ukulele. You might too. Move your strumming hand up and down the neck until you find the spot that is easiest for you. Just make sure you leave enough room for your playing hand. Remember, playing your ukulele is supposed to be fun and comfortable. Finding the perfect place to strum your ukulele will make things easier on you.

Rest your index finger against the top string of your ukulele. Now slowly and very lightly move your finger down all of the strings. The fingernail of your index finger should lightly brush against all of the strings and you should hear them loud and clear. Don't press down on the strings when you strum. Just lightly move your finger over them.

If you have long fingernails, it might be more difficult to strum. Sometimes long fingernails can get caught on the strings. You might need to clip them.

Now trying bringing your index finger back up. This time you won't be using your fingernail. Just use the soft tip of your finger and lightly move your finger up all of the strings.

If your index finger gets caught on the strings, keep trying until it moves over the strings nice and smooth. Practice strumming down and up.

Strumming your ukulele is powerful. You can make your ukulele louder by strumming harder. Give it a try, but not too hard. You don't want to break the strings!

You might find it easier to strum with your thumb. Give it a try. Use the side of your thumb to lightly brush down the strings the same way.

If strumming with your thumb is easier, then use your thumb. Playing the ukulele is supposed to be fun and easy. Do what works best for you!

The Playing Hand

Your playing hand is the hand that will be dancing all over the neck of the ukulele. Your four fingers will be used to press the strings against the fretboard. Your thumb will be used to brace your hand on the back of the ukulele neck like this. It is almost like you are going to be pinching the ukulele neck between your fingers and thumb.

The position of your fingers and your thumb on the back of the neck will change all the time. Do what feels comfortable.

This part can be tricky to master. It may even make the tips of your fingers or your wrist a little sore. If this happens to you, just take a break and try stretching out your playing hand. I like to open my hand like I am about to give someone a huge high five and then slowly make a fist. I do this four to five times in a row. This helps get the blood flowing to all of my fingers and helps to loosen them up a bit.

Holding the strings against the fretboard in the right place is very important. If you press the string too close the fret like in the image below, the note won't be clear and crisp. It might not even make a sound.

If you press the string too far away from the fret, it may be too hard to keep it pressed against the fretboard.

Try to keep your finger close to the middle.

Fret

Fret

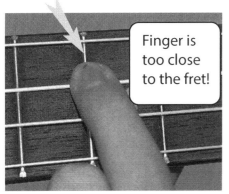

Practice holding down each string in different places on the neck using different fingers on your playing hand. Go ahead, let your fingers walk all over the neck of your ukulele.

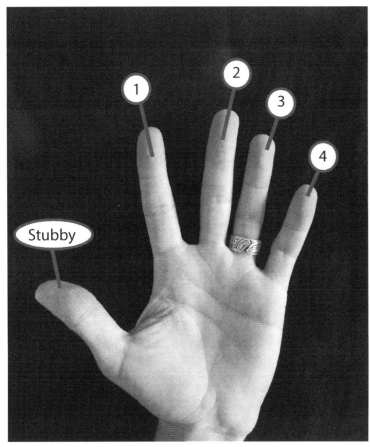

Let's give each one of the fingers on your right hand a name. This will make it easier for me to tell you how to play your ukulele. Let's use a number because numbers are easier to remember. Your pointer finger will now be called the 1st finger. Your middle finger will now be called your 2nd finger. Your ring finger will now be called your 3rd finger and your pinky finger will now be called your 4th finger. Your thumb doesn't get a name, but if you want to go ahead and give your thumb its own name, then go for it! I call mine Stubby because it is smaller than the rest of my fingers.

This is where your hands finally get to work together. Your playing hand will press a string or strings against the fretboard while your strumming hand strums those strings. It can be a little tricky getting your hands to work together like a team, but practice makes everything easier.

Try to keep your playing hand as relaxed and as comfortable as possible. It will take a little bit of practice getting your playing hand used to this.

Learning how to play the ukulele takes time. Slow and steady is the key here. Pretty soon, you will be able to make beautiful music and hold your ukulele for hours!

Low Notes VS High Notes

Knowing the difference between low notes and high notes is very important. The words low and high don't refer to the volume of the notes either. There is a big difference here. Low volume would be a tiny little whisper. HIGH VOLUME WOULD BE SOMEONE SHOUTING!

When I think of low notes, I think of a big old frog bellowing at the lake. When I think of high notes, I think of a bird singing in the morning sunshine.

Understanding high and low notes on your ukulele is easy. A low pitch note is the C or THIRD string on your ukulele.

A higher pitch note would be the A or FIRST string of your ukulele.

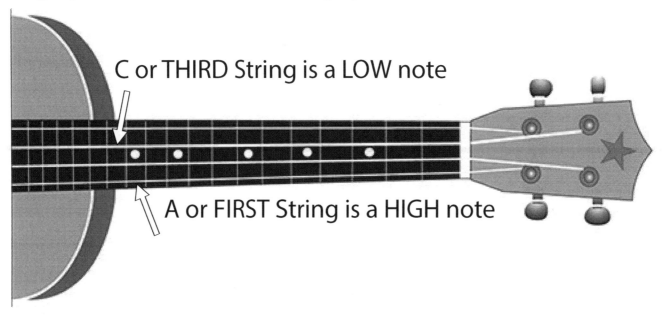

C or THIRD String is a LOW note

A or FIRST String is a HIGH note

Here is another awesome secret. The notes get higher in pitch as you work your way up the neck or towards the sound hole of your ukulele. Let's give it a try.

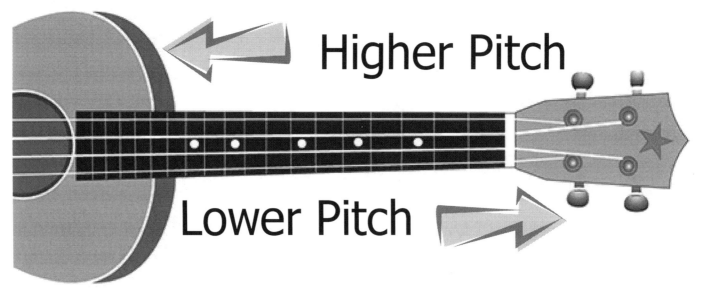

Higher Pitch

Lower Pitch

Use your thumb to strum the FOURTH or G string on the ukulele. You don't even need to hold the string. Just play it open. Go ahead strum just that one note. Listen to it. Now mute the string with the palm of your strumming hand by lightly resting your hand on the string.

FOURTH or G string played open

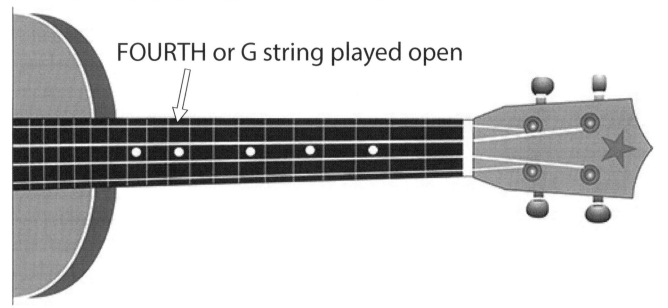

Use your 1st or index finger to press down the FOURTH string on the second fret. Remember to keep your finger as close to the middle of the frets as possible. Strum that string with the index finger or thumb of your strumming hand.

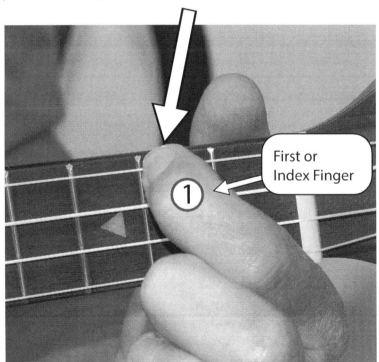

First or Index Finger

Move your first finger towards the sound hole to the next empty space on the neck and try again. Now move your finger up to the next empty space and try again. Did you notice how the pitch gets higher every time you move your 1st finger towards the sound hole? This is the difference in low pitch notes and high pitch notes. Now move your finger up to the next empty space and try again. Did you notice how the pitch gets higher every time you move your 1st finger higher up the neck? This is the difference in low pitch notes and high pitch notes.

Try this same thing on every string and notice how the sound changes. Now you are really making music. Good job! Practice with different playing fingers on the neck. You need to get every finger used to pressing down the strings on the fretboard, even your little pinky or 4th finger.

Chords

Anytime you play more than two notes at the same time on your ukulele, you are playing a chord. You already know that your hands need to work together like a team. Now the fingers on your playing hand will also have to work together like a team by holding down more than one string at a time. This is how you play chords and chords will make your ukulele sing loud and proud!

Playing chords will require some practice on your part, but the more you practice, the better you will be at playing your ukulele. I will give you plenty of great picture examples to make it easy to understand where your playing fingers should be and which strings you should be strumming. You will also learn how to read chord charts. Let's get ready to make some music!

Chord Charts Explained

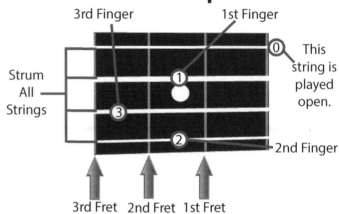

Wow! There is a lot of stuff going on in that chord chart isn't there? Chord charts are pretty easy to understand though. On the left side of the chord chart it tells you which strings to strum. In this example, you would be strumming every string on the ukulele.

The bottom of the chord chart tells you where the chord is played on the neck of the ukulele. In this example, the chord is played on the second and third frets.

The right side of the chord chart tells you which strings should be played open. Do you remember what it means to play an open string? It means you DO NOT press the string down on the fretboard.

You may have also noticed some circles with numbers in the middle on the fretboard. Do you remember when we gave each finger on your playing hand a number?

These numbers on the chord chart represent which playing finger should be holding the string down on the fretboard.

For each chord explanation, I will show you a chord chart and a real life picture to help you understand exactly how to play the chord. You will be making beautiful music in no time.

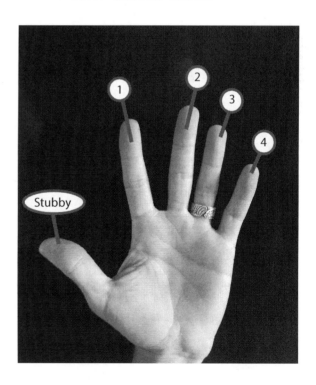

The first chords we are going to learn are called Major chords. Major chords sound happy! Let's take a look at the easiest chord to play on the ukulele.

C Major Chord

The C chord is my favorite because it is so easy to play. You only need to use one finger to hold down one note. The rest of the strings are all played open. I like to use my second finger to hold down the string but you can use any finger. You are not going to believe how easy it is to play this chord!

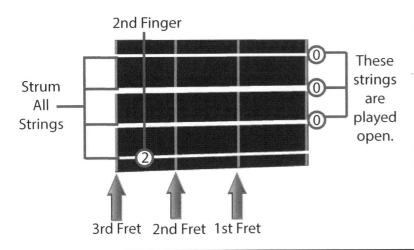

A Major Chord

The A Major chord is easy too. You will be holding down two strings and playing two strings open. Here are four examples of the A Major chord.

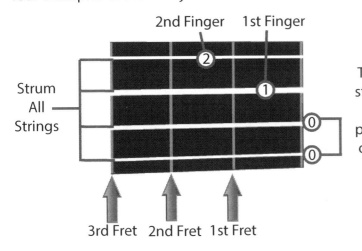

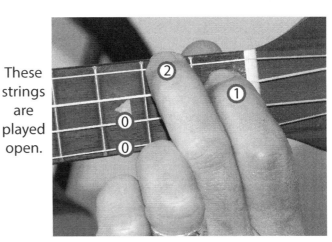

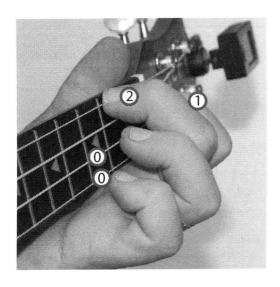

Page 18

F Major Chord

The F Major chord is a lot like the A Major chord. You will be using the same fingers to make this chord but your first finger will be holding down a different string.

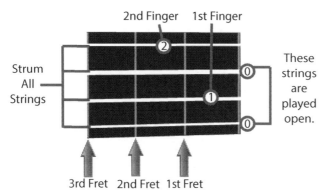

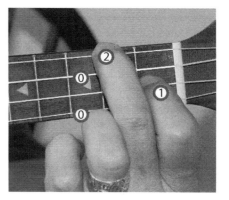

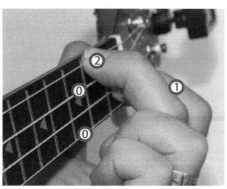

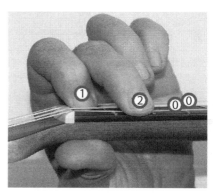

G Major Chord

The G chord brings in a new finger from your playing hand. You will be using your first, second and third fingers to make the G chord.

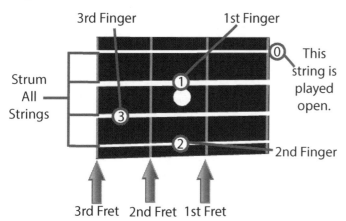

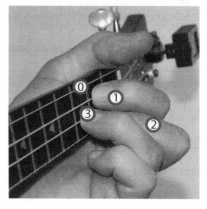

D Major Chord

The D Major chord will use three fingers from your playing hand. All three fingers will hold down three strings on one fret. I like to use my second, third and fourth fingers to make this chord, but you can use your first, second and third if you want. Look at the images below.

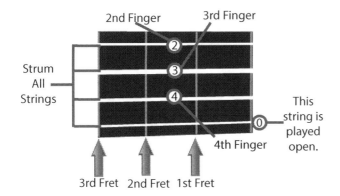

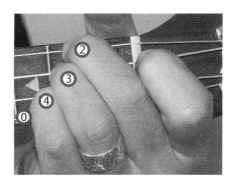

B Major Chord

The B Major chord will use three fingers from your playing hand but one of them has to hold two notes at the same time. Your index or FIRST finger will will be holding down two strings at once. This is also the first chord that is played a little higher up the neck. This chord will take a little bit of practice.

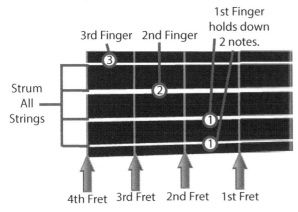

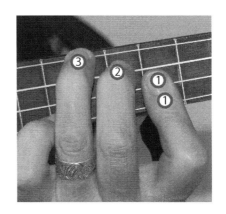

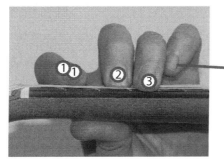

Notice how the FOURTH or PINKY finger is not touching any strings?

E Major Chord

The E Major chord is the first chord that will use all four fingers from your playing hand as a team. You won't be playing any open strings with this chord. This is a chord that will take some practice.

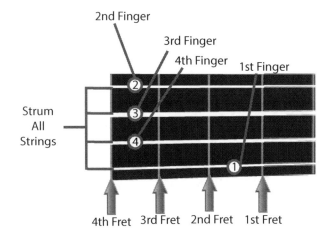

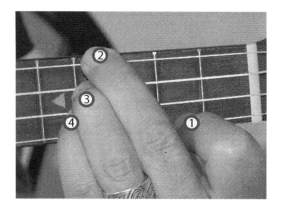

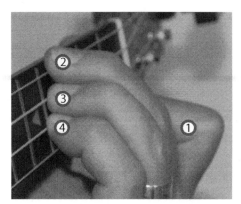

Congratulations! You have made it through all the Major chords in this book. You should be proud of yourself. You now know how to make beautiful music with your ukulele. Stand up and take a bow. You deserve it, but it is up to you to keep practicing. Try to practice each day for 10 minutes. You have put in a lot of work to make it this far through the book. Take a break. When you are ready to come back, we will work on Minor chords.

Now it is time to look at MINOR chords. Minor chords sound kind of sad but they are an important part of the music world. The first minor chord we are going to learn is really easy. You only use one finger from your playing hand. You can use your FIRST or SECOND finger. Take a look.

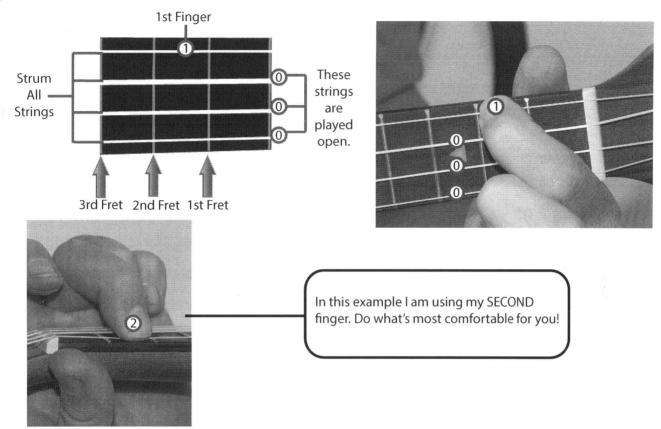

In this example I am using my SECOND finger. Do what's most comfortable for you!

C Minor Chord

The C MINOR chord will use three fingers from your playing hand. All three fingers will hold down three strings on one fret. I like to use my second, third and fourth fingers to make this chord, but you can use your first, second and third if you want. Look at the images below.

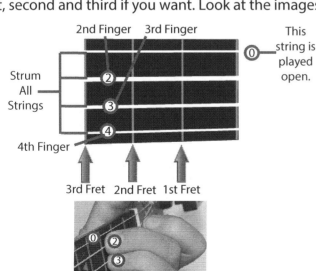

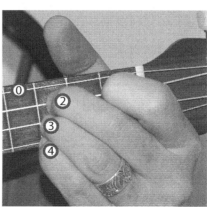

D Minor Chord

The D MINOR chord will use three fingers from your playing hand. Your PINKY or FOURTH finger will not be holding down any strings. Look at these images.

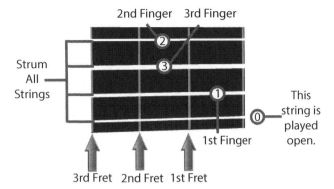

2nd Finger   3rd Finger

Strum All Strings

This string is played open.

1st Finger

3rd Fret   2nd Fret   1st Fret

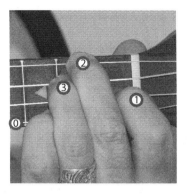

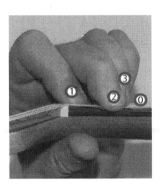

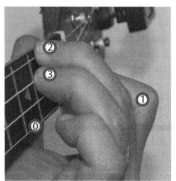

E Minor Chord

The E MINOR chord will use three fingers from your playing hand. All three fingers will hold down three strings on three different frets. Your PINKY or FOURTH finger won't be used. Look at the images below.

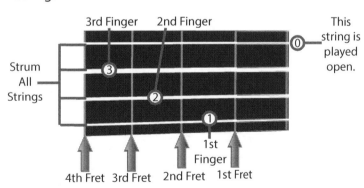

3rd Finger   2nd Finger

Strum All Strings

This string is played open.

1st Finger

4th Fret   3rd Fret   2nd Fret   1st Fret

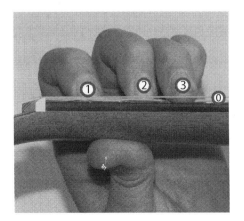

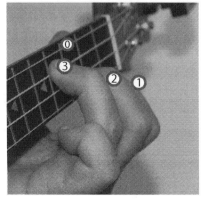

The B MINOR chord is going to be the most difficult to master, but don't let that bother you. It is difficult because you must use your INDEX or first finger to hold down three strings on one fret while holding the FOURTH string down with your THIRD finger. It is okay if you can't manage to get this chord on your first try. Just do your best and with enough practice the B MINOR chord will become easy.

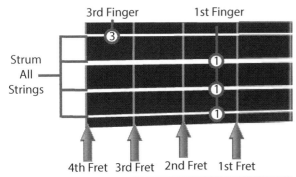

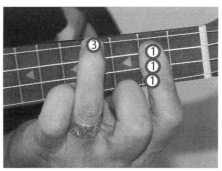

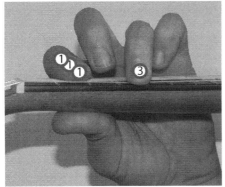

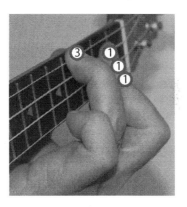

Congratulations! You have made it through the entire book. You should be very proud of yourself. Stand up and give yourself a round of applause. Parents, if you have been following along with your child, congratulate them and give them a pat on the back.

It is now up to you to practice everything you learned. Practice those chords and start playing them one after another. Mix them all up, and have fun. That's how you make your own music!

The more you practice, the better you will get. Playing your ukulele may seem hard at first. That's okay. I know mine was really hard to play when I first started playing, but I noticed that each day I practiced, I got better. Now I no longer practice my ukulele. I just play it.

There may be days when you look at your ukulele and think to yourself, "I don't feel like practicing." That's okay too. We all have days when we just don't want to pick up the ukulele and make it happy. But remember this, you can't get better at playing ukulele without practicing. Try to practice at least 10 minutes a day. The more you practice, the better you will get!

Thanks!

I would like to thank you for reading my book. I hope you enjoyed it and most importantly, I hoped it helped you learn how to play your ukulele. I am here to help you. If you don't understand any part of this book, email me. I will do my best to help you understand! My email address is:

wordsaremything@gmail.com

Don't forget to post a review and tell everyone what you thought of my book and have fun playing your ukulele!

Made in the USA
Columbia, SC
15 November 2017